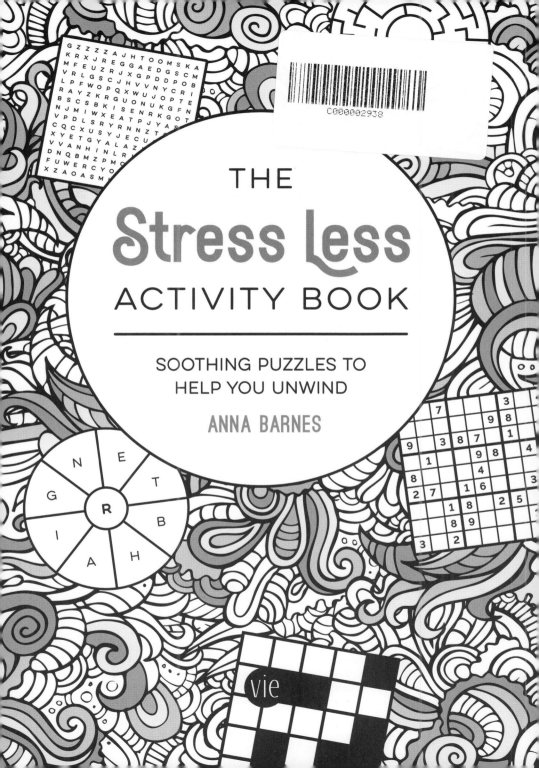

THE
Stress Less
ACTIVITY BOOK

SOOTHING PUZZLES TO
HELP YOU UNWIND

ANNA BARNES

vie

THE STRESS LESS ACTIVITY BOOK

Text by Pascale Duguay

An Hachette UK Company
www.hachette.co.uk

Vie Books, an imprint of Summersdale Publishers
Part of Octopus Publishing Group Limited
Carmelite House
50 Victoria Embankment
LONDON
EC4Y 0DZ
UK

www.summersdale.com

Printed and bound in China

ISBN: 978-1-83799-339-0

Substantial discounts on bulk quantities of Summersdale books are available to corporations, professional associations and other organizations. For details contact general enquiries: telephone: +44 (0) 1243 771107 or email: enquiries@summersdale.com.

Disclaimer
Neither the author nor the publisher can be held responsible for any injury, loss or claim – be it health, financial or otherwise – arising out of the use, or misuse, of the suggestions made herein. This book is not intended as a substitute for the medical advice of a doctor or physician. If you are experiencing problems with your physical or mental health, it is always best to follow the advice of a medical professional.

INTRODUCTION

With constant pressure to do and be more, it's no wonder that stress levels are at an all-time high, so why not take a moment to bring some peace into your life with this collection of relaxing puzzles and activities?

Solving puzzles is the perfect way to lower stress as it helps to improve mood, boost memory and reduce anxiety. In these pages, you will discover calming exercises, grounding mantras and relaxing breathing techniques to help you stress less, as well as a great selection of puzzles such as pairs games, crosswords, word searches, anagrams and sudokus. You can also unwind by colouring soothing images, focusing on the sound and texture of the pencil as you take your mind away from your worries.

Keep this book handy and turn to its pages whenever you feel the need to detach and decompress, and enjoy these rejuvenating activities that are certain to have you feeling calmer and more relaxed in no time.

CROSSWORD

SOOTHING GARDEN

Across

4. A canvas bed suspended by cords (7)

5. A reclining chair that supports the legs (7)

6. An object used to attract singing visitors (4, 6)

Down

1. Plants that add colour and feed bees (11)

2. A decorative ornament that uses water (8)

3. A roofed structure offering open views (6)

MAZE

Focus your mind on this activity, taking deep, mindful breaths as you trace a path through the maze. Allow your worries to float away with every swipe and swish of your pencil, embracing this moment of calm. Remember, if you feel your mind wandering, simply bring your attention back to the activity.

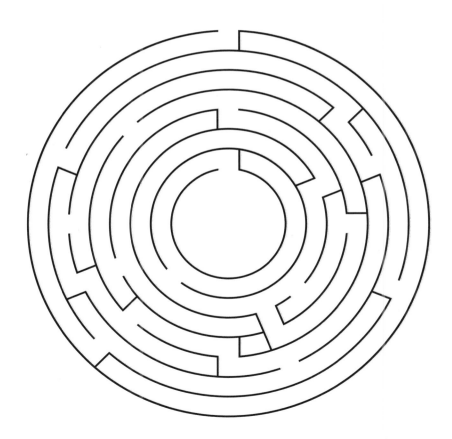

WORD SEARCH

A RELAXING PLAYLIST

```
G Z Z Z Z A J H T O O M S K A
K R X J R E G G A E D G S C M
M F E U Z R J X G P D D P O B
V R L G S C J H V V N Y C R I
L P F W O P Q X W U J O P T E
R A Y Z K R G U O N U K G F N
B S C S B K I S E N R K G O T
N J M I W X E A T P J Y A S M
V P D L S R Y R N N Z T C J U
C Q C X U S Y J E C U G Z D S
X Y E T G Y A L A Z H W I V I
V V A N H I N L R L T A U L C
D N Q B M Z P M C F T F N K W
F U W E R C Y O S Q N E Z T E
X Z A O A S M K G B H E Y G S
```

AMBIENT MUSIC

CLASSICAL

COUNTRY

GREGORIAN CHANTS

NATURE SOUNDS

REGGAE

SMOOTH JAZZ

SOFT ROCK

ZEN

SPOT THE DIFFERENCE

Can you find the ten differences between these two pictures?

DOT-TO-DOT

Join the dots to find the mystery image!

WORD LADDER

Change **CALM** into **MOOD** by altering one letter at a time to make a new word on each step of the ladder:

CALM
MOOD

ANAGRAMS

Rearrange these letters to reveal practices that will quiet your mind.

FAIR INFO MATS   _____

AN OMIT DIET   _____

GUT TIRADE   _____

PAIRS GAME

Match up the pairs of lotus flowers. The first one has been done for you.

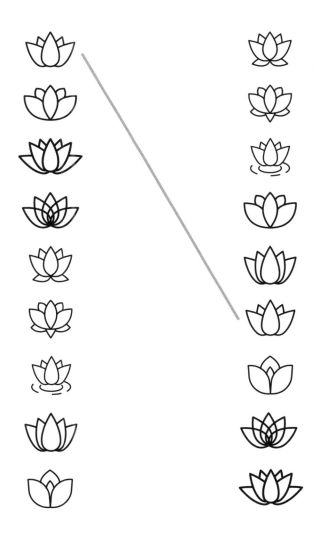

BREATHING EXERCISE

09

Consciously controlling your breathing encourages your mind to slow, your heart to steady and your body to calm down. Try this exercise to guide your breath, helping you to relax and feel more peaceful. It's as simple as one, two, three.

1. Place your finger at the starting point. Trace the lines of the shape as you inhale deeply through your nose.

2. Breathe in for as long as you find comfortable, counting to four, six or eight while following the pattern. At the top of the count, hold your breath and pause your finger.

3. When you feel ready, exhale slowly through your nose, expelling the air and any worries you have as you complete the shape.

Repeat this exercise to help you relieve stress and reclaim your calm.

STARTING
POINT

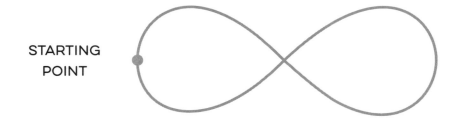

COUNTING CONUNDRUM

🐱 + 🐱 = 26

🐾 + 🐟 = 25

🐟 + 🐱 = 31

🐱 = ?   🐟 = ?   🐾 = ?

SUDOKU

Complete the following grid by filling in the empty boxes with the missing numbers. Each number can only appear once in a row, column or box.

		4	1
	1		
	2		4
	4	3	2

MISSING WORDS

Fill in the blank space to make two compound words or phrases:

SURF		WALK
SKY		READING
MOVIE		OWL

TRACKWORD

Find as many words of four or more letters as you can by moving from one square to the next in any direction, without going through any letter square again. Can you find the nine-letter word hidden in the square?

G	N	I
T	U	R
R	U	N

I BREATHE DEEPLY
AND FEEL MY
BODY RELAX

WORD WHEEL

See how many words of four or more letters you can make, using each letter only once. Each word must use the central letter. Can you find a word that uses all of the letters?

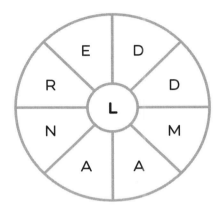

WORD LADDER

Change **FULL** into **MOON** by altering one letter at a time to make a new word on each step of the ladder:

FULL
MOON

WORD SEARCH

PICNIC DAY

```
S  N  O  I  H  S  U  C  G  K  R  S  J  A  B
R  F  L  R  J  M  K  P  B  T  E  J  H  H  R
X  Y  P  C  E  O  Y  L  J  I  T  D  O  Z  E
D  Z  E  F  T  F  A  Y  C  F  H  L  J  C  E
T  H  U  Z  K  N  R  A  O  I  G  E  Z  N  Z
T  A  A  P  K  O  C  E  S  L  U  V  I  G  E
A  M  Q  E  H  I  E  U  S  H  A  B  O  X  K
K  P  T  U  L  Z  A  N  L  H  L  U  E  J  T
O  E  O  E  T  Z  Y  A  I  U  M  Y  F  V  Z
H  R  D  J  F  U  J  Q  A  H  F  E  P  V  J
C  W  I  R  I  Z  C  I  U  V  S  B  N  G  Z
H  C  S  X  I  Y  T  V  J  G  W  N  R  T  H
H  N  K  T  W  K  D  W  P  P  J  U  W  S
M  E  C  V  S  W  G  J  X  A  U  H  E  S  H
B  C  B  Q  O  E  J  C  U  L  Y  N  B  Z  C
```

BLANKET	HAMPER
BREEZE	LAUGHTER
CUSHIONS	REFRESHMENTS
DELICACIES	SUNSHINE
DOZE	

DOT-TO-DOT

Join the dots to find the
mystery image!

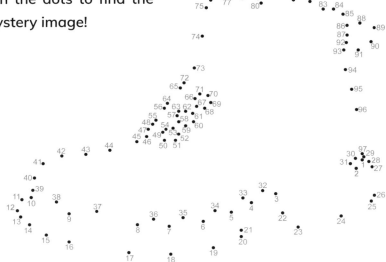

ANAGRAMS

Rearrange these letters to reveal things you might see on a
mountain hike.

SAW MODE   _____

TALL WAFERS   _____

HUMOR MOSS   _____

TRACKWORD

Find as many words of four or more letters as you can by moving from one square to the next in any direction, without going through any letter square again. Can you find the nine-letter word hidden in the square?

E	T	C
R	T	H
S	S	E

SUDOKU

Complete the following grid by filling in the empty boxes with the missing numbers. Each number can only appear once in a row, column or box.

		1	3
1		4	2
3	1		
		3	

CROSSWORD

READING TOOLS

Across

2. A device for reading in the dark (4)

4. Some people like to read while listening to _ _ _ _ _ (5)

5. A place where people go to buy books (9)

6. A piece of furniture to display and store books (8)

Down

1. An accessory for those who can't see up close (7)

3. An item used to mark one's place in a book (8)

MAZE

Can you help Mia find her notebook?

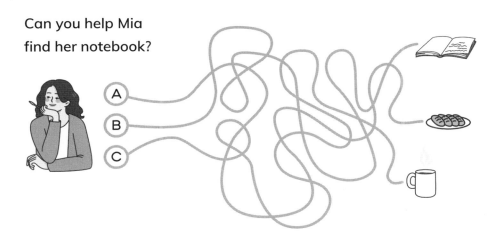

A

B

C

WORD LADDER

Change **PAGE** into **WORD** by altering one letter at a time to make a new word on each step of the ladder:

PAGE
WORD

CALMING EXERCISE

STREAM OF CONSCIOUSNESS

Allowing yourself to write freely, putting your thoughts and feelings to paper without judgement, helps to clear out and focus your mind. Try writing everything that is on your conscience right now to relieve stress and soothe your headspace.

_____

_____

_____

_____

_____

_____

_____

_____

_____

_____

SPOT THE DIFFERENCE

Can you find the ten differences between these two pictures?

COUNTING CONUNDRUM

☂ + ☂ + ☂ = 75

☂ − ⚫ − ⚫ = 15

⚫ × ★ = 50

☂ + ⚫ + ★ = ?

ANAGRAMS

Rearrange these letters to reveal things you can find on the beach.

FIST RASH _____

ASHES SELL _____

CROP LOOKS _____

PAIRS GAME

Match up the pairs of hearts. The first one has been done for you.

WORD LADDER

Change **HAPPY** into **DANCE** by altering one letter at a time to make a new word on each step of the ladder:

HAPPY
DANCE

ANAGRAMS

Rearrange these letters to reveal things that will make you laugh.

SILK ETC _____

WICK RACES _____

MID CANOE _____

I LET GO OF
MY WORRIES

WORD WHEEL

See how many words of four or more letters you can make, using each letter only once. Each word must use the central letter. Can you find a word that uses all of the letters?

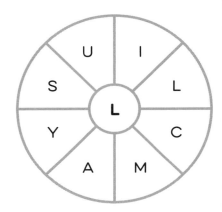

WORD LADDER

Change **HEAR** into **BELL** by altering one letter at a time to make a new word on each step of the ladder:

HEAR
BELL

COUNTING CONUNDRUM

🌰 + 🌰 + 🌰 = 60

🌰 + 🥜 + 🥜 = 50

🥜 − 🍃 − 🍃 = 3

🍃 + (🍃 × 🌰) − 🥜 = ?

SUDOKU

Complete the following grid by filling in the empty boxes with the missing numbers. Each number can only appear once in a row, column or box.

3			
4	1		
2		4	1
1	4	3	

CROSSWORD

JOURNALLING

Across

4. Journalling can help you feel _ _ _ _ _ _ _ (7)

6. A writing tool with a reservoir or cartridge allowing ink to flow continuously to the nib (8, 3)

Down

1. Thin sheets made from the pulp of trees (5)

2. Felt-tip pens that come in many colours (7)

3. A good place to journal at night (3)

5. A book for writing daily personal events and experiences (5)

SPOT THE DIFFERENCE

Can you find the ten differences between these two pictures?

BREATHING EXERCISE

Consciously controlling your breathing encourages your mind to slow, your heart to steady and your body to calm down. Try this exercise to guide your breath, helping you to relax and feel more peaceful. It's as simple as one, two, three.

1. Place your finger at the starting point. Trace the lines of the shape as you inhale deeply through your nose.

2. Breathe in for as long as you find comfortable, counting to four, six or eight while following the pattern. At the top of the count, hold your breath and pause your finger.

3. When you feel ready, exhale slowly through your nose, expelling the air and any worries you have as you complete the shape.

Repeat this exercise to help you relieve stress and reclaim your calm.

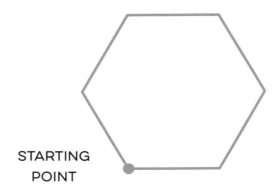

STARTING
POINT

WORD SEARCH

AT THE PARK

```
G P Z K Z K E G U U X G L X A
G N Y O Y N N N Z W L A D K U
A A I Z W K B I Z E Y T Z C O
T J V L O U K Y Y E T H W D K
K U O P L M P A O C K E A N Q
E D D G Z O F L E P O R U C F
D C D Z G J R P Z C N I M M E
F R I S B E E T O S S N Q Q S
K J O Q P A R N S Q T G S K G
N P C C B H C Z A V Y S B O N
Z V B F X E E T D G T U Z M G
F V L G R S E H C N E B J N Q
Y S G T S Y M Q S J B M I Q R
S Q U I R R E L S R P W U Z K
H P E V S X K M O L S K I P V
```

BENCHES	PLAYING
CONCERT	SQUIRRELS
FRISBEE TOSS	STROLLING
GATHERINGS	SWING
JOGGER	

TRACKWORD

Find as many words of four or more letters as you can by moving from one square to the next in any direction, without going through any letter square again. Can you find the nine-letter word hidden in the square?

O	F	L
B	O	E
K	S	H

SUDOKU

Complete the following grid by filling in the empty boxes with the missing numbers. Each number can only appear once in a row, column or box.

4	3	2	
	1	3	4
1	2		3
3	4		

CROSSWORD

Across

2. To run at a gentle pace (3)

4. The practice of emptying one's mind or thinking calming thoughts (10)

5. She takes frequent _ _ _ _ _ _ throughout the day (6)

6. To walk in a leisurely way (6)

Down

1. A stretching exercise (4)

3. To write down one's thoughts or experiences in a book (7)

MAZE

Can you help the bird fly to its birdhouse?

WORD LADDER

Change **BIRD** into **SONG** by altering one letter at a time to make a new word on each step of the ladder:

BIRD
SONG

WORD SEARCH

BIRD WATCHING

```
S F X Y C E F E T K C E C S J
N R M N A X G U H J C A T I Q
Q M A K Y A H F G U N E C N I
V Y A L M F E D I A Y K P G M
C G S U U E X G L C X E N I T
Z M L H D C J I F R K T V N V
P P V I D M O D E E R F Z G F
Q I N K Q X O N U J R D I R F
D G Q Z E P S X I E B V D Z W
U N O Z E Y C O D B Q C N G K
V H E N T X R X E U X X Z J E
W A O S K V V B G C A H W T O
C O U R T I N G T P B B F Z I
B Q Y W U S N Q Q O B M T G O
M K S K L M J M E Y V G O N K
```

BINOCULARS   NESTS

COURTING   PECK

FEEDING   PLUMAGE

FLIGHT   SINGING

FREEDOM

SPOT THE DIFFERENCE

Can you find the ten differences between these two pictures?

COUNTING CONUNDRUM

🧶 × 🧶 = 100

🪡 + 🪡 − 🧶 = 34

🧦 − 🪡 = 38

🧦 − (🧶 ÷ 2) + 🪡 = ?

ANAGRAMS

Rearrange these letters to reveal creative activities.

CUPS GLINT _____

MICE CARS _____

HOG HOP PARTY _____

PAIRS GAME

Match the pairs of stacked pebbles. The first one has been done for you.

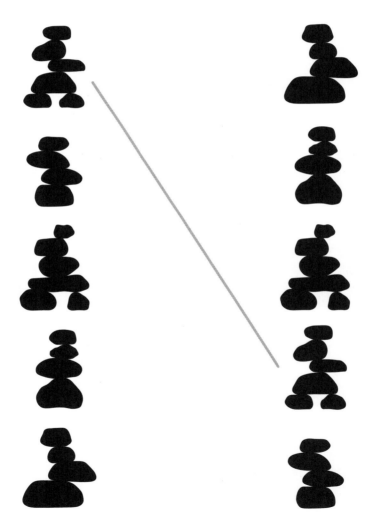

WORD LADDER

Change **HEART** into **BEATS** by altering one letter at a time to make a new word on each step of the ladder:

HEART
BEATS

ANAGRAMS

Rearrange these letters to reveal fitness accessories.

BULB MELD   _____

MAYO TAG   _____

SWEAT BLOTTER   _____

CALMING EXERCISE

THOUGHT CLOUDS

Assessing the severity and impact of your stresses can help you to identify which feelings need to be addressed first, making the process of working through them more manageable. Try noting down your thoughts in the clouds below, writing the "weightier" worries inside the larger shapes to determine which could be tackled right now.

I DESERVE TO FEEL
JOY, COMFORT
AND CALM

COUNTING CONUNDRUM

🌈 × ❄️ = 28

❄️ × 💧 = 20

💧 + ❄️ = 9

🌈 = ?   ❄️ = ?   💧 = ?

SUDOKU

Complete the following grid by filling in the empty boxes with the missing numbers. Each number can only appear once in a row, column or box.

4		3	2
2	3		1
3	2		4
	4	2	

DOT-TO-DOT

Join the dots to find the mystery image!

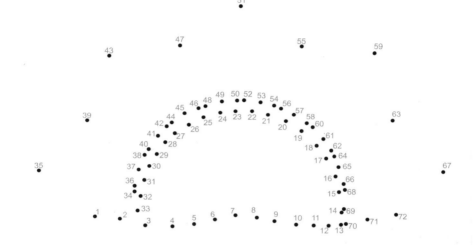

MISSING WORDS

Fill in the blank space to make two compound words or phrases:

SILK		MUSIC
HANGING		WEAVING
SPRING		SLIDE

SPOT THE DIFFERENCE

Can you find the ten differences between these two pictures?

MAZE

Focus your mind on this activity, taking deep, mindful breaths as you trace a path through the maze. Allow your worries to float away with every swipe and swish of your pencil, embracing this moment of calm. Remember, if you feel your mind wandering, simply bring your attention back to the activity.

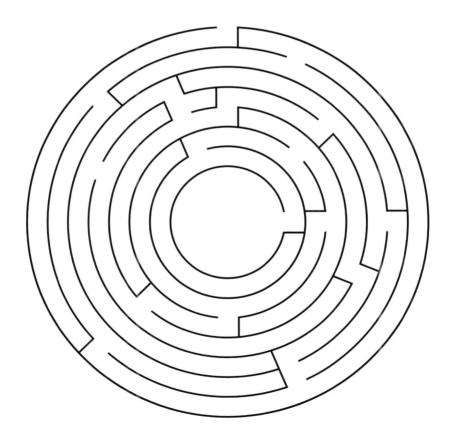

WORD SEARCH

BEDTIME RITUALS

```
M Q J H S E N S G P O K G F J
T E Z H L G E M L Y M K N M O
N B D M G L F L Z J W Q I K U
D J F I G X X H H A B G D H R
I K R G T A U C B M G O A D N
E R U C N A Z A J A Z G E K A
M N W S U D T Y M S X T R N L
S D E E P B R E A T H I N G L
J A E T E L I M O M A H C E I
V I S U A L I Z I N G X T Z N
S K O T L D I T Z I S N E A G
N W F X I C P S O X Z X H M B
G K I L Z N G W Q N V Y C C O
G N J C W Q S K K O Z D Q O M
H T L K K U X G V L E H Z C V
```

BATH	PYJAMAS
CHAMOMILE TEA	READING
DEEP BREATHING	SNUGGLES
JOURNALLING	VISUALIZING
MEDITATE	

56

DOT-TO-DOT

Join the dots to find the mystery image!

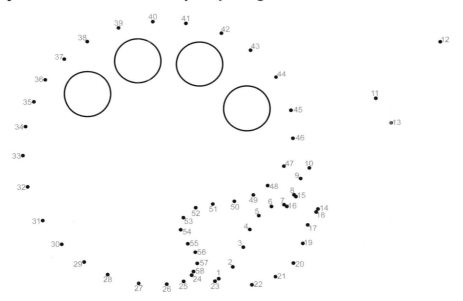

ANAGRAMS

Rearrange these letters to reveal drawing tools.

PETALS _____

ARCH COLA _____

PEN SHARER _____

TRACKWORD

Find as many words of four or more letters as you can by moving from one square to the next in any direction, without going through any letter square again. Can you find the nine-letter word hidden in the square?

A	T	N
M	E	E
A	Z	M

SUDOKU

Complete the following grid by filling in the empty boxes with the missing numbers. Each number can only appear once in a row, column or box.

4		2	1
2			
3	2		
1	4	3	

CROSSWORD

CHILLING ON A HOT DAY

Across

2. A large juicy fruit with red flesh (10)

3. A drink made from lemon juice and sweetened water (8)

5. A frozen treat usually eaten in a cone or dish (3, 5)

6. A partially frozen drink made with crushed ice and fruit-flavoured syrup (7)

Down

1. A thick drink made with fresh or frozen fruit (8)

4. An Italian-style ice cream (6)

BREATHING EXERCISE

Consciously controlling your breathing encourages your mind to slow, your heart to steady and your body to calm down. Try this exercise to guide your breath, helping you to relax and feel more peaceful. It's as simple as one, two, three.

1. Place your finger at the starting point. Trace the lines of the shape as you inhale deeply through your nose.

2. Breathe in for as long as you find comfortable, counting to four, six or eight while following the pattern. At the top of the count, hold your breath and pause your finger.

3. When you feel ready, exhale slowly through your nose, expelling the air and any worries you have as you complete the shape.

Repeat this exercise to help you relieve stress and reclaim your calm.

STARTING
POINT

WORD SEARCH

OUT FOR LUNCH

```
S  E  Y  N  S  O  S  M  E  A  N  D  E  R  U
R  T  K  X  R  L  T  P  J  H  J  T  E  K  B
P  F  R  T  L  O  A  R  N  Y  S  P  C  I  X
J  Q  S  E  B  H  E  S  Z  A  O  L  E  P  I
Y  I  J  O  T  F  R  B  T  S  Q  T  W  O  U
B  D  P  E  V  C  T  Q  E  M  O  X  U  K  C
Q  Y  D  N  X  Y  H  M  G  Q  S  L  L  D  O
V  R  N  R  J  Z  S  I  D  V  U  P  U  Z  M
C  J  U  Y  Z  K  T  Q  N  T  B  L  L  S  P
S  R  U  O  V  A  L  F  D  G  Q  C  R  B  A
M  F  S  G  V  V  O  E  Q  I  A  Q  L  B  N
C  N  I  R  Z  A  T  C  F  G  W  C  X  W  I
E  Y  I  U  I  U  S  S  L  D  H  P  D  X  O
D  K  M  H  H  H  W  V  Z  N  O  K  I  H  N
T  V  H  X  T  X  O  Y  H  L  X  L  S  S  S
```

BISTRO	SAVOUR
COMPANIONS	STRETCHING
FLAVOURS	TASTE
MEANDER	TREATS
REPOSE	

62

SPOT THE DIFFERENCE

Can you find the ten differences between these two pictures?

COUNTING CONUNDRUM

$$\text{bike} \times 2 = 24$$

$$\text{helmet} \times 3 = 12$$

$$\text{pump} \times 4 = 20$$

$$\text{bike} + \text{helmet} + \text{pump} = ?$$

ANAGRAMS

Rearrange these letters to reveal things to enjoy on a bike ride.

GAS TONIC   _____

AROMA NAP   _____

EAR NUT   _____

PAIRS GAME

Match the pairs of towels. The first one has been done for you.

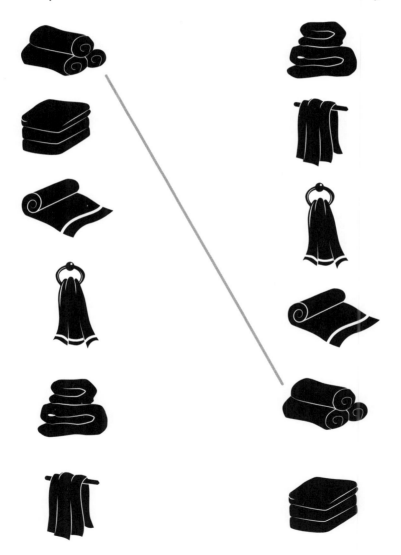

I CAN OVERCOME
ANYTHING

CROSSWORD

COMFORT FOODS

Across

4. Contains a high percentage of cocoa (4, 9)

6. Meat, fish or vegetables cooked slowly in a covered pot (4)

Down

1. Baked in a round dish with a flaky crust (3)

2. Best eaten fresh from the oven and spread with butter (5)

3. Served in a bowl with crackers on the side (4)

5. Baked layers of wide pasta strips, tomato sauce and cheese (7)

TRACKWORD

Find as many words of four or more letters as you can by moving from one square to the next in any direction, without going through any letter square again. Can you find the nine-letter word hidden in the square?

N	D	R
O	E	F
W	L	U

WORD LADDER

Change **GOOD** into **LIFE** by altering one letter at a time to make a new word on each step of the ladder:

	GOOD
	LIFE

COUNTING CONUNDRUM

$$\boxed{} + \boxed{} + \boxed{} = 18$$

$$(\boxed{} \times \boxed{}) + \bigcirc = 41$$

$$\bigcirc + (\bigcirc \times \bigcirc) = 55$$

$$(\bigcirc \times \boxed{}) \div \bigcirc = ?$$

SUDOKU

Complete the following grid by filling in the empty boxes with the missing numbers. Each number can only appear once in a row, column or box.

4	1		
2	3		
	4	3	2
		1	

DOT-TO-DOT

Join the dots to find the mystery image!

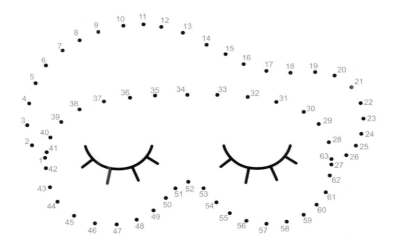

MISSING WORDS

Fill in the blank space to make two compound words or phrases:

LOVE		BELT
SAFETY		BALL
SUN		SHOW

CALMING EXERCISE

TO-DO LIST

Jotting down everything you have to do helps you to achieve tasks and organize your life. Try making a list of all the things you need to do today, this week or this month, ensuring you also consider time for self-care and hobbies to decompress your mind.

PAIRS GAME

Match up the pairs of musical notes. The first one has been done for you.

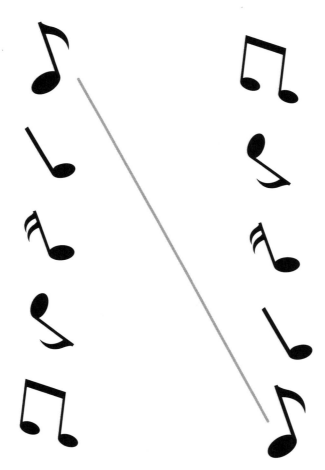

MAZE

Can you help Aidan make his way to the pool?

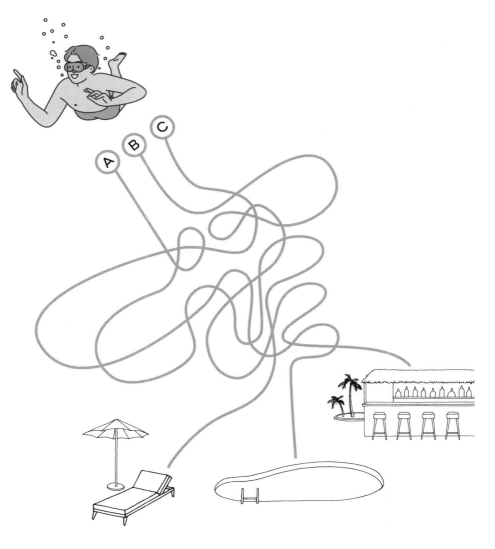

DOT-TO-DOT

Join the dots to find
the mystery image!

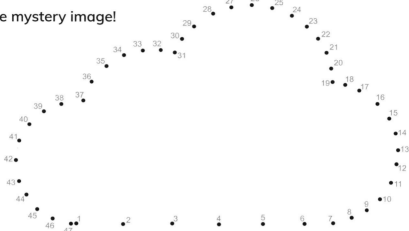

ANAGRAMS

Rearrange these letters to reveal shapes you might see while
cloud watching.

IN LAMAS   _____

EEL POP   _____

NICE TOURS   _____

SPOT THE DIFFERENCE

Can you find the ten differences between these two pictures?

CROSSWORD

BEST PLACES TO READ

83

Across

3. A roofed shelter along the outside of a house (7)

5. A structure built in the branches of a tree (9)

6. A public garden with benches (4)

Down

1. A piece of furniture also known as a couch (4)

2. A cushioned platform next to panes of glass (6, 4)

4. A sandy surface next to a large body of water (5)

DOT-TO-DOT

Join the dots to find
the mystery image!

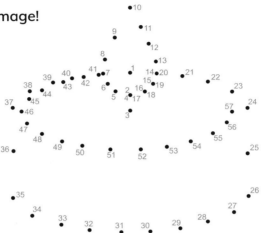

MISSING WORDS

Fill in the blank space to make two compound words or phrases:

BATH		CAKE
PEACE		POST
OPEN		PORT

WORD SEARCH

FUN WITH PETS

```
P  I  B  G  V  B  G  E  G  S  J  I  X  C  E
A  P  Y  B  N  V  X  N  I  B  L  G  A  I  L
M  Z  X  C  F  I  I  V  L  B  I  E  P  G  D
P  S  S  Z  Z  S  Y  Q  C  J  V  D  E  T  D
E  K  C  C  S  D  K  A  F  W  P  M  I  P  U
R  S  Y  E  H  S  Z  G  L  H  S  U  N  S  C
R  A  R  T  I  E  K  V  N  P  A  I  I  X  J
B  A  T  X  Q  V  H  C  A  H  C  C  H  I  B
C  S  M  U  Z  P  E  P  I  O  W  D  U  V  L
R  R  M  X  S  U  D  L  S  R  H  S  R  Y  Y
P  L  V  Q  R  X  Z  T  X  Y  T  W  B  X  L
U  X  X  D  B  Q  U  R  U  N  G  Y  Z  C  D
Y  J  U  T  V  M  B  H  U  B  E  K  H  Y  U
J  B  Y  Y  E  S  E  S  S  I  K  K  S  E  A
V  B  D  S  L  O  Y  D  Q  X  W  M  T  V  H
```

CARESSING	PLAYING
COSTUMES	RUN
CUDDLE	SLEEP
KISSES	TRICKS
PAMPER	

81

SPOT THE DIFFERENCE

Can you find the ten differences between these two pictures?

$$\text{kite} + \text{wind} = 25$$

$$\text{wind} - \text{kite} = 15$$

$$\text{wind} \div \text{kite} = 4$$

$$\text{wind} = ? \qquad \text{kite} = ?$$

ANAGRAMS

Rearrange these letters to reveal things that float in the air.

BABBLE OPUS   _____

LOAN SLOB   _____

ATE FRESH   _____

BREATHING EXERCISE

Consciously controlling your breathing encourages your mind to slow, your heart to steady and your body to calm down. Try this exercise to guide your breath, helping you to relax and feel more peaceful. It's as simple as one, two, three.

1. Place your finger at the starting point. Trace the lines of the shape as you inhale deeply through your nose.

2. Breathe in for as long as you find comfortable, counting to four, six or eight while following the pattern. At the top of the count, hold your breath and pause your finger.

3. When you feel ready, exhale slowly through your nose, expelling the air and any worries you have as you complete the shape.

Repeat this exercise to help you relieve stress and reclaim your calm.

STARTING
POINT

I INVITE AND
ACCEPT PEACE
INTO MY LIFE

CROSSWORD

BREAK TIME

Across

4. A puzzle containing interlocking pieces (6)

5. A hot drink made with plants (6, 3)

6. To create a picture on paper with a pencil (4)

Down

1. A card game played by one person (9)

2. A short sleeping session (3)

3. To fill an image using pencils or crayons (6)

WORD WHEEL

See how many words of four or more letters you can make, using each letter only once. Each word must use the central letter. Can you find a word that uses all of the letters?

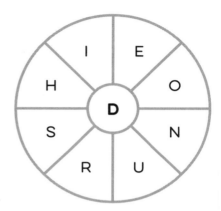

WORD LADDER

Change **SOUL** into **FOOD** by altering one letter at a time to make a new word on each step of the ladder:

SOUL
FOOD

PAIRS GAME

Match up the pairs of islands. The first one has been done for you.

DOT-TO-DOT

Join the dots to find the mystery image!

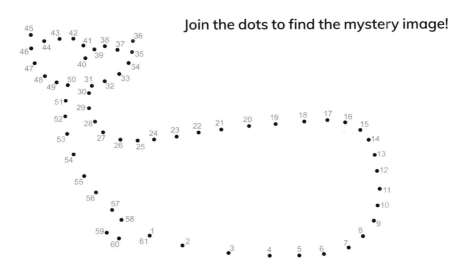

MISSING WORDS

Fill in the blank space to make two compound words or phrases:

WHOLE		ONE
APPLE		PAN
POETRY		DUNK

SPOT THE DIFFERENCE

Can you find the ten differences between these two pictures?

MAZE

Focus your mind on this activity, taking deep, mindful breaths as you trace a path through the maze. Allow your worries to float away with every swipe and swish of your pencil, embracing this moment of calm. Remember, if you feel your mind wandering, simply bring your attention back to the activity.

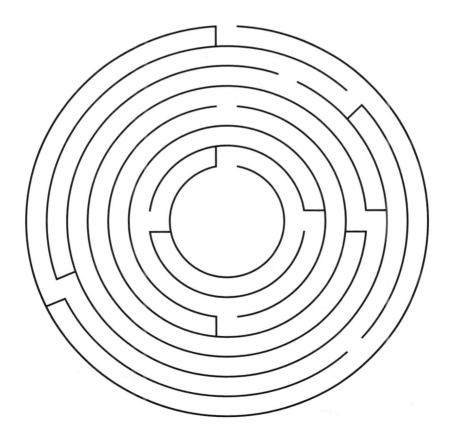

WORD SEARCH

WINTER ESCAPADE

```
T X Z C D R E H Y I O Q W D C
A A P M Y A B C C D O O L M P
K E Z I I A V E A G Y O W X W
Y D L Y Q T S M K L Y T R O A
K D X C J K T N N U P R A W N
R P S D A U F E D A S E S F R
L D A T B Z M T N W E E R Z F
X I I V O P A U N S O E B I H
M N E T A L O C O H C T O H F
G C K D K J M J S J N I O A E
A D W W Y H Z W H H E Y T L P
A E D D Q Q O B C W N H S A E
F L J I Z N S K I S H Y R U Y
K S I M S O X U D V A K G Z Y
Z T D Y U W V O B E A K Q A N
```

BOOTS	PARKA
FIREPLACE	SKIS
HOT CHOCOLATE	SLED
ICE SKATING	SNOWSHOES
MITTENS	

DOT-TO-DOT

Join the dots to find the mystery image!

ANAGRAMS

Rearrange these letters to reveal things to take with you on a weekend getaway.

GALS SENSUS   _____

GET BOAT   _____

A CREAM   _____

CALMING EXERCISE

POSITIVE SPIN

Taking an uncomfortable feeling, such as stress, and looking for the positive in the situation can help you to reframe your thoughts, alleviating anxiety. Write down four things that are worrying you, then try finding something good about each: a new-found gratitude for something, perhaps, or a challenge you can overcome.

TRACKWORD

Find as many words of four or more letters as you can by moving from one square to the next in any direction, without going through any letter square again. Can you find the nine-letter word hidden in the square?

I	G	O
N	W	L
M	E	L

WORD LADDER

Change **SOFT** into **TONE** by altering one letter at a time to make a new word on each step of the ladder:

SOFT
TONE

DOT-TO-DOT

Join the dots to find the mystery image!

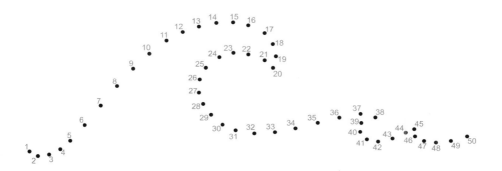

MISSING WORDS

Fill in the blank space to make two compound words or phrases:

DRAW		ORCHESTRA
BLUE		PULL
TREASURE		NUT

CROSSWORD

BE KIND TO YOURSELF

Across

3. Look on the bright side, stay
_ _ _ _ _ _ _ _ (8)

5. Be merry, _ _ _ _ _ often (5)

6. Praise your achievements, be your own _ _ _ _ _ leader (5)

Down

1. Move your body, _ _ _ _ _ _ _ _ every day (8)

2. Let go of shame, _ _ _ _ _ _ _ your mistakes (7)

4. Engage in fun activities, make time to _ _ _ _ (4)

SUDOKU

Complete the following grid by filling in the empty boxes with the missing numbers. Each number can only appear once in a row, column or box.

	1	2	4
			3
1	3		2
	4		1

MAZE

Can you help Anna find her sunhat?

A

B

C

COUNTING CONUNDRUM

110

📷 + 📷 + 📷 = 42

📷 + 📖 + 📖 = 38

📖 + 📷(tripod) + 📷(tripod) = 32

(📷(tripod) × 📖) − 📷 = ?

ANAGRAMS

111

Rearrange these letters to reveal things you can do with photos.

BARK SCOOP   _____

AVOID ROBINS   _____

CLOG SALE   _____

WORD LADDER

Change **FREE** into **TIME** by altering one letter at a time to make a new word on each step of the ladder:

FREE
TIME

ANAGRAMS

Rearrange these letters to reveal types of retreats.

SELL NEWS _____

INFESTS _____

WIN GRIT _____

WORD SEARCH

MOVIE NIGHT

```
F U P D N Y U B O T P T R X L
I R F X U S W E A T P A N T S
E T I P S E R E V N U H I D P
F F H U D G I Y S A G S T T R
Y F L Q M M V S S I X B L Y A
T X C U P N E H G V T U B Z W
E G S L F N X G F R Q A Y O L
K P L T K F L F H R N E M T V
N O S R U E Y M N R O C P O P
A L A P S D Z S C M F T O W Y
L D C Y U W L I O V O E U Y A
B F D A G U H D V C X C N T R
V X X A A W R C D I K F M U N
Y P I E K J V G G Y K S U O B
Y V G C J Z O S I I L V D O R
```

BLANKET   RESPITE

DARKNESS   ROMCOM

FLUFFY SOCKS   SPRAWL

GIGGLES   SWEATPANTS

POPCORN

CROSSWORD

ENERGIZING SCENTS

Across

3. A yellow citrus fruit (5)

4. A light brown Asian root spice that can be grated or chopped (6)

5. A type of mint often used in candy (10)

Down

1. A herb containing the names of a flower and a female (8)

2. A spice from the bark of a tree, grated or used as sticks in drinks and desserts (8)

5. A tree with needle-shaped leaves (4)

WORD WHEEL

See how many words of four or more letters you can make, using each letter only once. Each word must use the central letter. Can you find a word that uses all of the letters?

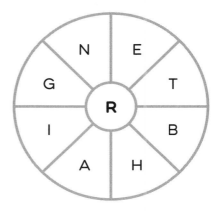

WORD LADDER

Change **REST** into **HEAL** by altering one letter at a time to make a new word on each step of the ladder:

REST
HEAL

BREATHING EXERCISE

Consciously controlling your breathing encourages your mind to slow, your heart to steady and your body to calm down. Try this exercise to guide your breath, helping you to relax and feel more peaceful. It's as simple as one, two, three.

1. Place your finger at the starting point. Trace the lines of the shape as you inhale deeply through your nose.

2. Breathe in for as long as you find comfortable, counting to four, six or eight while following the pattern. At the top of the count, hold your breath and pause your finger.

3. When you feel ready, exhale slowly through your nose, expelling the air and any worries you have as you complete the shape.

Repeat this exercise to help you relieve stress and reclaim your calm.

STARTING
POINT

CROSSWORD

SPENDING TIME WITH FRIENDS

Across

1. A long walk in the wilderness (4)

5. A trip involving sleeping in a tent (7)

6. A meal where each of the guests brings a dish (7)

Down

2. A machine that plays the tunes of songs while people take turns singing the words (7)

3. A two-wheeled vehicle propelled by pedals (7)

4. A place where movies are shown (6)

MAZE

Focus your mind on this activity, taking deep, mindful breaths as you trace a path through the maze. Allow your worries to float away with every swipe and swish of your pencil, embracing this moment of calm. Remember, if you feel your mind wandering, simply bring your attention back to the activity.

WORD SEARCH

BREAKFAST IN BED

```
S W X R C Q X Q R Z P P P E O
W V Y E R Q S C U Q G Q C U F
O I V D O W K E J D T I Y H Y
L V B Q I U L B Y E U J A F I
L L K R S E Q O V J R S R H F
I Q B C S T R U H G O Y T R H
P S Q C A A D Z Q F Z R U I K
N D U V N W H F V Y Y I B C O
V U L I T L A M Q R T G O O S
M A R M A L A D E S O J F S I
Q K O S O C R K A S I S L Y T
G Q Q W Z J H L Z D M K E S M
K J N I D T A P L J W W L M I
Y K Y N B D Q G O Z X R T D I
C S I R H E B I O Z I R H C Z
```

CROISSANT	PILLOWS
DUVET	ROSE
FRUIT SALAD	TRAY
JUICE	YOGHURT
MARMALADE	

SPOT THE DIFFERENCE

Can you find the ten differences between these two pictures?

DOT-TO-DOT

Join the dots to find the mystery image!

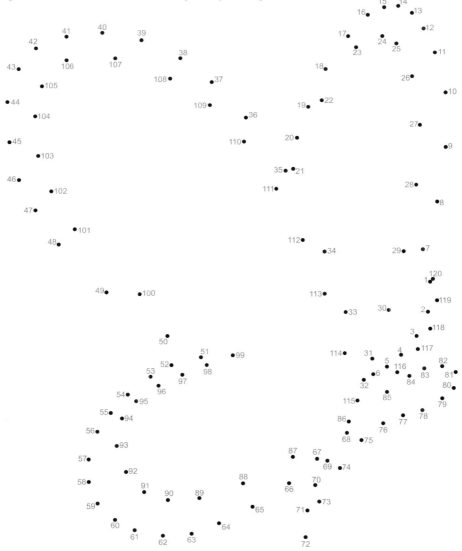

WORD LADDER

Change **COOL** into **RAIN** by altering one letter at a time to make a new word on each step of the ladder:

COOL
RAIN

ANAGRAMS

Rearrange these letters to reveal types of refreshing rainfall.

LINK REPS   _____

MINI FEST   _____

EIGHT WHORLS   _____

PAIRS GAME

Match up the pairs of starfish. The first one has been done for you.

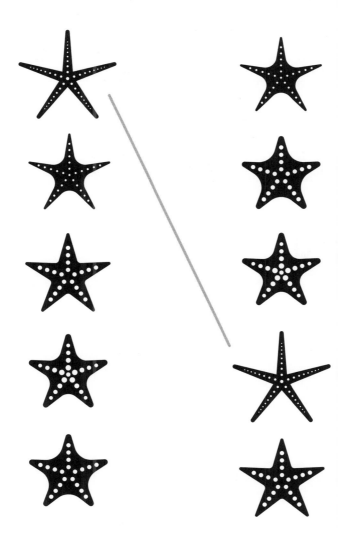

COUNTING CONUNDRUM

$$\text{(mask)} + \text{(mask)} + \text{(mask)} = 30$$

$$\text{(mask)} + \text{(dreamcatcher)} + \text{(dreamcatcher)} = 50$$

$$\text{(dreamcatcher)} \div \text{(moon)} = 5$$

$$\text{(mask)} + \text{(dreamcatcher)} + \text{(moon)} = ?$$

SUDOKU

Complete the following grid by filling in the empty boxes with the missing numbers. Each number can only appear once in a row, column or box.

2		1	4
	4	2	3
4			
		4	2

MISSING WORDS

Fill in the blank space to make two compound words or phrases:

TENT		VAULT
CAMP		PROOF
RIVER		NOTE

TRACKWORD

Find as many words of four or more letters as you can by moving from one square to the next in any direction, without going through any letter square again. Can you find the nine-letter word hidden in the square?

S	A	G
S	E	E
E	N	R

CALMING EXERCISE

WORRY BALLOONS

Visualizing your worries floating away offloads your mind and lightens your headspace, helping you to feel less stressed. Try writing a word for each of your concerns in the hot air balloons, then imagine them drifting into the distance.

I AM SAFE

WORD WHEEL

See how many words of four or more letters you can make, using each letter only once. Each word must use the central letter. Can you find a word that uses all of the letters?

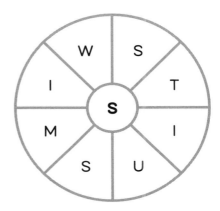

WORD LADDER

Change **WATER** into **LOVER** by altering one letter at a time to make a new word on each step of the ladder:

WATER
LOVER

WORD SEARCH

SPA DAY

```
T O K L X U H B K K M D Z E F
X G H X Q G A G J N A N Q S I
Q M R N S T G O K I S S K S L
V L F C H R F W T K S G A E Q
G P E R F J H M O S A A G N A
I Q O E S N C R Z G G O T T Z
Z B L A I C A F S N E U R I A
E R U C I D E P Z I G R Q A H
D N U I P J J Y H W J V V L Z
A L F R J E Z Z N O Q W G O S
B Y R R Z A J P M L U W M I F
Y U Y U F D K K X G F W X L K
E A R O M A T H E R A P Y S U
J J D C N F I F G L A I I P O
Y J Q N S X U L Q C Z V A Q O
```

AROMATHERAPY

BATHROBE

ESSENTIAL OILS

FACIAL

GLOWING SKIN

MASSAGE

PEDICURE

SAUNA

SCRUB

DOT-TO-DOT

Join the dots to find the mystery image!

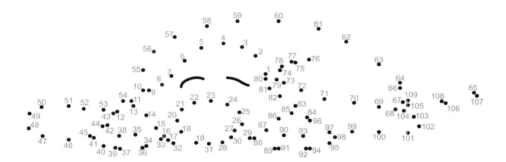

ANAGRAMS

Rearrange these letters to reveal types of comfy clothing.

OHIO ED   _____

EGG SLING   _____

RIGHT HINTS   _____

TRACKWORD

Find as many words of four or more letters as you can by moving from one square to the next in any direction, without going through any letter square again. Can you find the nine-letter word hidden in the square?

E	S	S
N	L	T
L	S	I

SUDOKU

Complete the following grid by filling in the empty boxes with the missing numbers. Each number can only appear once in a row, column or box.

	1		4
4		3	
1			
	4	1	

CROSSWORD

UNWINDING IN THE COUNTRYSIDE

Across

3. A small, soft, red fruit studded with seeds (10)

4. A large four-legged animal with a flowing mane (5)

6. An activity that uses a rod and bait (7)

Down

1. A colourful insect with two pairs of large wings (9)

2. A wooded area (6)

5. A narrow boat with pointed ends propelled by a paddle (5)

MAZE

Can you help Joshua pick the right shoes for his evening jog?

WORD LADDER

Change **CHEERY** into **DREAMS** by altering one letter at a time to make a new word on each step of the ladder:

CHEERY
DREAMS

SPOT THE DIFFERENCE

Can you find the ten differences between these two pictures?

COUNTING CONUNDRUM

$$\text{🐝} + \text{🐝} + \text{🐝} = 15$$

$$\text{🐝} + \text{🍯} + \text{🍯} = 55$$

$$\text{🍯} - \text{⬡} = 5$$

$$\text{⬡} + (\text{🍯} \div \text{🐝}) = ?$$

ANAGRAMS

Rearrange these letters to reveal summer insects.

HAP PROGRESS   _____

CHARM ON   _____

THRONE   _____

BREATHING EXERCISE

Consciously controlling your breathing encourages your mind to slow, your heart to steady and your body to calm down. Try this exercise to guide your breath, helping you to relax and feel more peaceful. It's as simple as one, two, three.

1. Place your finger at the starting point. Trace the lines of the shape as you inhale deeply through your nose.

2. Breathe in for as long as you find comfortable, counting to four, six or eight while following the pattern. At the top of the count, hold your breath and pause your finger.

3. When you feel ready, exhale slowly through your nose, expelling the air and any worries you have as you complete the shape.

Repeat this exercise to help you relieve stress and reclaim your calm.

STARTING
POINT

PAIRS GAME

Match up the pairs of suns. The first one has been done for you.

WORD LADDER

Change **WING** into **SOAR** by altering one letter at a time to make a new word on each step of the ladder:

WING
SOAR

ANAGRAMS

Rearrange these letters to reveal types of birds.

SLUG ALE   _____

BRING HIM MUD   _____

CROOKED PEW   _____

I EMBRACE

MYSELF FULLY

WORD WHEEL

See how many words of four or more letters you can make, using each letter only once. Each word must use the central letter. Can you find a word that uses all of the letters?

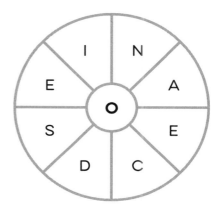

WORD LADDER

Change **SURF** into **WAVE** by altering one letter at a time to make a new word on each step of the ladder:

SURF
WAVE

COUNTING CONUNDRUM

✍️✍️ + ✍️✍️ + ✍️ = **20**

📖✍️ 📖✍️ + ✍️ = **10**

⌨️ + 📖✍️ = **18**

⌨️⌨️ + (📖✍️ × ✍️) = **?**

SUDOKU

Complete the following grid by filling in the empty boxes with the missing numbers. Each number can only appear once in a row, column or box.

		1	2
	1		3
	2	3	4
			1

CROSSWORD

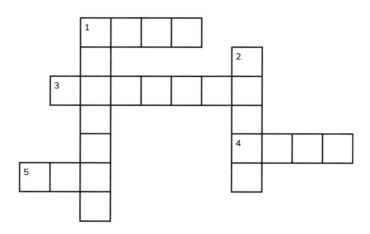

Across

1. A tailless amphibian that leaps and croaks (4)

3. A leaping insect that chirps (7)

4. Moisture that falls from the sky (4)

5. A nocturnal bird (3)

Down

1. A flying insect that flashes in the dark (7)

2. Fixed luminous points in the night sky (5)

SPOT THE DIFFERENCE

Can you find the ten differences between these two pictures?

WORD SEARCH

NATURE RETREAT

```
S  C  F  U  E  C  B  G  H  K  S  X  L  H  Z
F  L  U  F  D  C  I  F  V  G  M  S  O  F  F
F  Y  I  U  N  D  O  G  E  F  V  T  O  A  K
C  W  C  A  Z  X  T  C  H  S  S  Y  U  J  P
J  R  B  G  R  E  R  G  A  P  W  N  A  N  A
E  I  U  N  S  T  R  N  R  B  A  L  K  E  A
D  A  C  N  N  P  D  I  E  B  I  Z  A  Q  U
C  O  U  A  G  B  N  K  X  W  X  N  P  B  B
N  S  F  T  B  G  Q  I  P  R  I  B  M  F  K
G  R  K  Q  D  B  X  B  L  M  Z  P  A  G  L
G  L  A  M  P  I  N  G  O  Z  Q  W  I  V  I
M  W  H  X  X  I  B  F  R  L  I  U  L  E  H
G  N  I  K  I  H  M  Q  I  F  A  Y  M  E  P
P  C  E  W  Y  L  O  P  N  W  Z  K  E  S  Q
V  C  K  A  F  A  X  B  G  U  X  L  T  A  T
```

BIKING	HIKING
ECO CABIN	HOT SPRING
EXPLORING	SUNSET
FAUNA	TRAILS
GLAMPING	

ANSWERS

01: hammock, lounger, bird feeder, wildflowers, fountain, gazebo

02:

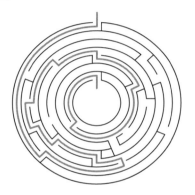

03:

04:

05:

06: balm, bald, bold, mold

07: affirmations, meditation, gratitude

08:

demand, derma, dermal, dram, drama, dream, lama, lame, lamed, lamer, leman, madden, madder, made, maenad, malar, male, mana, mandela, mandrel, mane, maned, mara, mare, marl, marled, mead, meal, mean, medal, medlar, mela, meld, mend, name, named, namer, ramen, realm, ream, remand

15: fill, mill, mild, mold, mood

10: 🐱 = 13 🐟 = 18 🐾 = 7

16:

11:

2	3	4	1
4	1	2	3
3	2	1	4
1	4	3	2

12: board, light, night

13: nine-letter word = nurturing; other words = guru, inurn, ring, ruin, ruing, rung, runt, truing, trug, turn

14: nine-letter word = dreamland; other words = adman, admen, alarm, alarmed, alderman, amen, amend, anadem, armed, daman, damar, dame, damn, damned,

17:

18: meadows, waterfalls, mushrooms

19: nine-letter word = stretches; other words = chest, chests, erst, ester, esters, etch, etches, hest, retch, retches, rets, sets, sett, setter, setters, stet, stretch, terse, tret

20:

4	2	1	3
1	3	4	2
3	1	2	4
2	4	3	1

21: lamp, music, bookstore, bookcase, glasses, bookmark

22: b

23: wage, wake, woke, wore

25:

26:  = 25 = 5 = 10

27: starfish, seashells, rock pools

28:

29: harpy, hardy, handy, dandy, dancy

30: tickles, wisecrack, comedian

31: nine-letter word = musically; other words = acyl, asci, aulic, call, calls, callus, calm, calmly, calms, cams, caul, caulis, cauls, cays, claim, claims, clam, clams, clay, clays, clumsily, clumsy, cull, cullis, culls, cully, culm, culms, cyma, cymas, lacy, laic, lilac, lilacs, macs, mica, miscall, muscly, music, musical, saucily, saucy, scaly, scam, scilla, scull, scum, sulci, sumac

32: bear, beat, belt

33: = 20 = 15 = 6

146

34:

3	2	1	4
4	1	2	3
2	3	4	1
1	4	3	2

35: relaxed, fountain pen, paper, markers, bed, diary

36:

38:

39: nine-letter word = bookshelf; other words = bole, boles, book, books, bosh, bosk, floe, floes, fobs, foes, fool, hobo, hobs, hole, holes, hoof, hose, kobo, kobs, koel, lobs, lose, oboe, oboes, oohs

40:

4	3	2	1
2	1	3	4
1	2	4	3
3	4	1	2

41: jog, meditation, breaks, stroll, yoga, journal

42: b

43: bind, wind, wing, sing

44:

45:

46: = 10 = 22 = 60

47: sculpting, ceramics, photography

48:

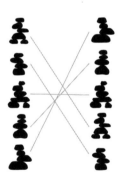

49: hears, heats

50: dumbbell, yoga mat, water bottles

52: = 7 = 4 = 5

53:

4	1	3	2
2	3	4	1
3	2	1	4
1	4	2	3

54:

55: sheet, basket, water

56:

57:

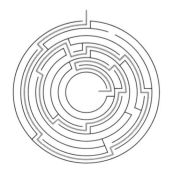

58:

59:

60: pastel, charcoal, sharpener

61: nine-letter word = amazement; other words = amaze, amen, ament, eaten, enema, mate, maze, meat, meet, meme, mete, tame, team, teem, teen, zeta

62:

4	3	2	1
2	1	4	3
3	2	1	4
1	4	3	2

63: watermelon, lemonade, ice cream, slushie, smoothie, gelato

65:

66:

67: 🚲 = 12　⛑ = 4　🚲 = 5

68: coasting, panorama, nature

69:

70: dark chocolate, stew, pie, bread, soup, lasagne

71: nine-letter word = wonderful; other words = doer, dole, done, dowel, dower, drew, enol, endow, enow, felon, fend, fled, flew, floe, flowed, flower, flue, lend, leno, lode, loden, lone, loner, lowed, nerd, node, noel, owed, redo, reflow, rend, wend, woeful, wolf, wolfed, wonder

72: wood, word, wore, wire, wife

73: ⬜ = 6   ⬭ = 5   ⬚ = 10

74:

4	1	2	3
2	3	4	1
1	4	3	2
3	2	1	4

75:

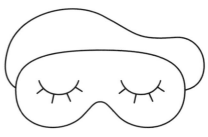

76: seat, net, flower

78:

79: c

80:

81: animals, people, countries

82:

83: veranda, treehouse, park, sofa, window seat, beach

84:

85: sponge, sign, air

86:

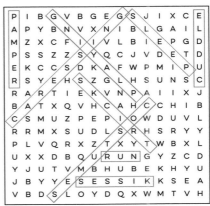

87:

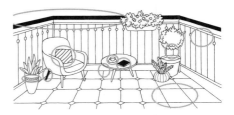

88: = 20 = 5

89: soap bubble, balloons, feathers

91: jigsaw, herbal tea, draw, solitaire, nap, colour

92: nine-letter word = nourished; other words = dehorn, dehorns, dinero, dino, dinos, doer, doers, does, done, dons, dose, dosh, dour, douse, douser, drone, drones, dronish, duos, enshroud, eons, euro, euros, heinous, hero, heroin, heron, herons, hideous, hods, hoed, hoer, hoers, hoes, hone, honed, hones, horde, hordes, horn, horned, horns, horse, horsed, hose, hosed, hoser, hosier, hound, hounder, hounds, hour, hours, houri, houris, house, housed, indorse, inhouse, inshore, ions, iron, ironed, irons, node, nodes, nods, noir, noire, noirs, noise, nori, nose, nosed, nosied, nourish, nous, odes, ones, onside, onus, ores, ours, redo, resound, rhino, rhinos, rode, rods, rose, rosed, rosied, round, roundish, rounds, rouse, roused, senior, shod, shoder, shoe, shone, shore, shored, shorn, shroud, snore, snored, sone, sore, sound, sounder, sour, soured, udon, udons, undo, undoes, unhorse, unhorsed, unshod

93: foul, fool

94:

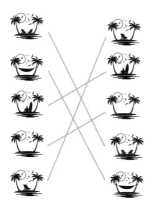

95:

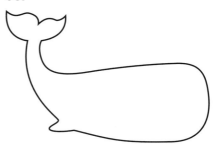

96: some, sauce, slam

97:

98:

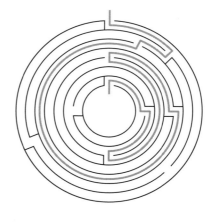

99:

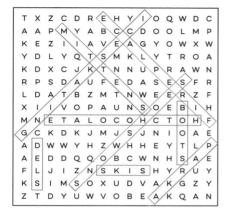

100:

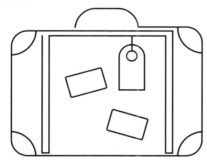

101: sunglasses, tote bag, camera

103: nine-letter word = mellowing; other words = glow, gown, mewl, owing, lowing, mellow, mewing, well, wine, wing

104: sort, sore, tore

105:

106: string, bell, chest

107: positive, laugh, cheer, exercise, forgive, play

108:

3	1	2	4
4	2	1	3
1	3	4	2
2	4	3	1

109: c

110: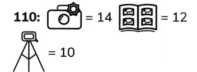

111: scrapbook, vision board, collages

112: fret, feet, feel, fell, tell, till, tile

113: wellness, fitness, writing

114:

```
F  U  P  D  N  Y  U  B  O  T  P  T  R  X  L
I  R  F  X  U  S  W  E  A  T  P  A  N  T  S
E  T  I  P  S  E  R  E  V  N  U  H  I  D  P
F  F  H  U  D  G  I  Y  S  A  G  S  T  T  R
Y  F  L  Q  M  M  V  S  S  I  X  B  L  Y  A
T  X  C  U  P  N  E  H  G  V  T  U  B  Z  W
E  G  S  L  F  N  X  G  F  R  Q  A  Y  O  L
K  P  L  T  K  F  L  F  H  R  N  E  M  T  V
N  O  S  R  U  E  Y  M  N  R  O  C  P  O  P
A  L  A  P  S  D  Z  S  C  M  F  T  O  W  Y
L  D  C  Y  U  W  L  I  O  V  O  E  U  Y  A
B  F  D  A  G  U  H  D  V  C  X  C  N  T  R
V  X  X  A  A  W  R  C  D  I  K  F  M  U  N
Y  P  I  E  K  J  V  G  G  Y  K  S  U  O  B
Y  V  G  C  J  Z  O  S  I  I  L  V  D  O  R
```

115: lemon, ginger, peppermint, rosemary, cinnamon, pine

116: nine-letter word = breathing; other words = abet, agent, ante, anti, aright, baht, bait, baiter, bant, banter, barite, bate, bath, bathe, bather, bathing, bating, beat, beating, bent, berating, berth, bertha, berthing, beta, bight, binate, birth, bite, biter, brat, breath, bright, brighten, earth, earthing, eating, eight, gait, gaiter, garnet, gate, gather, gent, giant, girth, gnat, granite, grant, grate, gratin, great, grit, habit, hairnet, hart, hate, hater, hating, heart, heat, heating, henbit, hint, inert, ingather, ingrate, inter, irate, neat, night, nitre, rant, rate, rating, rebating, rent, retain, retina, right, rite, tahr, tang, tare, taring, tarn, tear, tearing, tern, than, thane, thar, their, then, thenar, thin, thing, tier, tiger, tine, tinea, ting, tinge, tire, train, triage, tribe, trine

117: best, beat, heat

119: hike, camping, potluck, karaoke, bicycle, cinema

120:

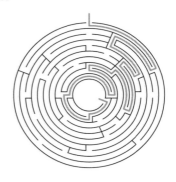

121:

```
S  W  X  R  C  Q  X  Q  R  Z  P  P  P  E  O
W  V  Y  E  R  Q  S  C  U  Q  G  Q  C  U  F
O  I  V  D  O  W  K  E  J  D  T  I  Y  H  Y
L  V  B  Q  I  U  L  B  Y  E  U  J  A  F  I
L  L  K  R  S  E  Q  O  V  J  R  S  R  H  F
I  Q  B  C  S  T  R  U  H  G  O  Y  T  R  H
P  S  Q  C  A  A  D  Z  Q  F  Z  R  U  I  K
N  D  U  V  N  W  H  F  V  Y  Y  I  B  C  O
V  U  L  I  T  L  A  M  Q  R  T  G  O  O  S
M  A  R  M  A  L  A  D  E  S  O  J  F  S  I
Q  K  O  S  O  C  R  K  A  S  I  S  L  Y  T
G  Q  Q  W  Z  J  H  L  Z  D  M  K  E  S  M
K  J  N  I  D  T  A  P  L  J  W  W  L  M  I
Y  K  Y  N  B  D  Q  G  O  Z  X  R  T  D  I
C  S  I  R  H  E  B  I  O  Z  I  R  H  C  Z
```

122:

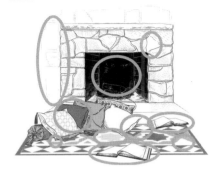

123:

124: coil, roil, rail

125: sprinkle, fine mist, light shower

126:

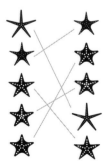

127: ⌷ = 10   ✦ = 20

☾ = 4

128:

2	3	1	4
1	4	2	3
4	2	3	1
3	1	4	2

129: pole, fire, bank

130: nine-letter word = eagerness; other words = ages, eager, ease, eases, erne, esse, gases, gasser, gees, geese, gene, genes, genre, genres, gens, ness, sage, sager, sages, seas, seen, seer, sees, sene, senega, sense, sere, sneer

132: nine-letter word = swimsuits; other words = imus, mist, miss, mists, must, smut, stum, stums, suit, suits, sumi, swim, swims, swum, wist, wits

133: later, laver

134:

139: strawberry, horse, fishing, butterfly, forest, canoe

140: c

141: cheers, cheeks, creeks, creaks, creams

135:

142:

136: hoodie, leggings, nightshirt

137: nine-letter word = stillness; other words = enlist, illness, ills, isle, isles, istle, lens, less, lest, list, lists, nest, nests, sell, sells, sill, silt, silts, slit, slits, stile, stiles, still, tile, tiles, till, tills

143: 🐝 = 5 🐝(hive) = 25

🍯 = 20

144: grasshopper, monarch, hornet

146:

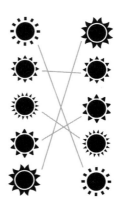

138:

3	1	2	4
4	2	3	1
1	3	4	2
2	4	1	3

147: wink, sink, sick, sock, soak

148: seagull, hummingbird, woodpecker

149: nine-letter word = oceanside; other words = aced, aces, acid, acids, acne, acned, acnes, adios, adonis, aeon, aeons, aide, aides, aids, anise, anode, anodes, anodic, ascend, aside, cads, candies, cane, caned, canes, canoe, canoed, canoes, cans, case, cased, casino, ciao, ciaos, coda, codas, dais, dance, dances, deacon, deacons, dean, deans, diocesan, idea, ideas, incase, incased, ocean, oceans, said, sand, sane, scad, scan, sedan, soca, soda

150: sure, cure, care, cave

151: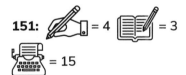

152

3	4	1	2
2	1	4	3
1	2	3	4
4	3	2	1

153: frog, cricket, rain, owl, firefly, stars

154:

155:

THE MINDFULNESS ACTIVITY BOOK

CALMING PUZZLES TO HELP YOU RELAX

ANNA BARNES

978-1-80007-679-2
PAPERBACK

Take a moment to unwind with this activity book, packed with calming puzzles, breathing exercises and colouring pages.

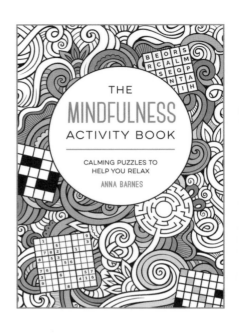

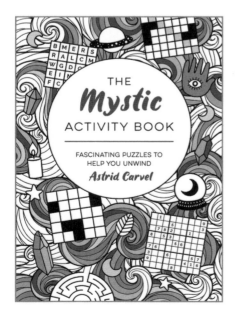

THE MYSTIC ACTIVITY BOOK

FASCINATING PUZZLES TO HELP YOU UNWIND

ASTRID CARVEL

978-1-80007-685-3
PAPERBACK

Discover the wonders of the paranormal with this collection of spellbinding puzzles and brain-training activities, here to focus your mind and inspire creativity.

IMAGE CREDITS

Have you enjoyed this book?
If so, find us on Facebook at
Summersdale Publishers, on Twitter/X
at **@Summersdale** and on Instagram and
TikTok at **@summersdalebooks** and get
in touch. We'd love to hear from you!

www.summersdale.com

In the process they helped each other to talk up salaries and perks over lunch tables (perhaps it's breakfast now).

(*Guardian*, 26 October 1986: 28)

Thus, as a general phenomenon, wages in the City of London have moved upwards, in many cases substantially. The City's average salaries are now well above those of the South East, and far above those of Britain as a whole (Table 4.9).

Table 4.8 Rates of pay for sample of financial jobs, City of London, 1987

Job	Lowest salary (£)	Highest salary (£)
Senior executive, corporate finance	50,000	150,000
Specialists in corporate finance	40,000	115,000
Equities market maker	25,000	100,000
Gilts salesperson	40,000	100,000
Fund manager	20,000	50,000
Fund manager – overseas equities	25,000	100,000
Bonds dealer	25,000	75,000
Swaps salesperson	21,000	82,250
Euronotes marketer	25,000	100,000
Sterling dealer	12,250	25,000
Senior sterling dealer	19,250	32,500
Bank operations manager	25,000	50,000
Company secretary	24,950	35,000
Bank chief accountant	24,500	40,000
Bank financial controller	39,950	60,000
Investment analyst	20,000	75,000
Economist	15,000	25,000
Lawyer	17,500	31,150

Source: Remuneration Economics (1987)

The movement upwards of salaries has been distributed (unequally) amongst four main groups. First of all, there were the directors and partners of the various City firms – the so-called 'icing'. These people were already well paid before the Big Bang. In 1985, 361 directors in forty-two companies earned more than £100,000 a year; twenty-four of them earned more than £250,000 a year (*Labour Research* 1986). These people's overall financial position was improved somewhat by the buying out of directors and partners of many City firms as the process of centralisation took place. Some of them walked away with sums of £1 million and more.

Second, there were the top managers and dealers – the so-called 'marzipan' layer. These people have begun to earn very substantial salaries. In 1985, before the Big Bang, only sixty-seven employees in fourteen companies earned more than £100,000 (with nine earning more than £250,000). In the period leading up to the Big Bang and after this the position has changed, especially if a person has skills in short supply.